SPACE GARBAGE

by Ruth Owen

PowerKiDS
press

New York

Published in 2015 by **The Rosen Publishing Group, Inc.**
29 East 21st Street, New York, NY 10010

Library of Congress Cataloging-in-Publication Data
Owen, Ruth.
Space garbage / by Ruth Owen.
p. cm. — (Objects in space)
Includes index.
ISBN 978-1-4777-5863-2 (pbk.)
ISBN 978-1-4777-5868-7 (6-pack)
ISBN 978-1-4777-5866-3 (library binding)
1. Space debris — Juvenile literature. 2. Space pollution — Juvenile literature.
I. Owen, Ruth, 1967-. II. Title.
TL1499.O94 2015
363.72—d23

Produced for Rosen by Ruby Tuesday Books Ltd
Editor for Ruby Tuesday Books Ltd: Mark J. Sachner
US Editor: Sara Antill
Designer: Emma Randall
Consultant: Kevin Yates, Fellow of the Royal Astronomical Society

Photo Credits:
Cover, 1, 7, 8, 11 (bottom), 13, 15 (top), 19, 21, 25, 29 © NASA; 5, 27 © Science
Photo Library; 11 (top), 14–15 © Shutterstock; 15 (bottom) © Jakub Halun
(Public Domain); 17 © Public Domain; 23 © European Space Agency (ESA).

Manufactured in the United States of America
CPSIA Compliance Information: Batch # CW15PK: For Further Information contact Rosen Publishing, New York, New York at 1-800-237-9932

CONTENTS

A JUNKYARD IN SPACE

Our Earth has a garbage problem. Vast areas of ground are needed so that household trash can be buried in landfill. The planet's oceans are becoming polluted with bottles, disposable coffee cups, and other plastic trash. But did you know that even the sky high above your head is filling with junk?

At the end of 2013, the U.S. space agency **NASA** reported that there were more than 500,000 pieces of space debris **orbiting** Earth. This human-made garbage includes old pieces of rockets used to launch spacecraft and **satellites** that are no longer in use.

Traveling at speeds of 17,500 miles per hour (28,000 km/h), these pieces of debris could potentially collide with spacecraft or the International Space Station (ISS). This could endanger the lives of astronauts and cause serious damage to hugely expensive spacecraft. Space debris can also seriously damage **space telescopes** or the satellites that we rely on to provide weather forecasts, cell-phone signals, GPS, and the Internet.

SPACE OBJECTS FACT FILE

Space garbage is also known as orbital debris, space junk, and space waste. It is any human-made object in orbit around Earth that no longer carries out a useful function.

This illustration is not to scale, but it shows how space debris might look as it orbits Earth.

AROUND AND AROUND

Our Earth is protected by a thick layer of gases called the **atmosphere**. High above Earth, the atmospheric gases become thinner until they eventually merge into space.

Earth's huge gravitational pull keeps smaller objects, such as space debris, in orbit around it. Most space debris orbits Earth in a Low Earth Orbit (LEO). This means the object is traveling at a height of between 100 and 1,250 miles (160 and 2,000 km) above Earth's surface. This is outside of the thickest part of Earth's atmosphere.

In time, pieces of debris suffer orbital decay. This means their orbits get closer and closer to Earth. Eventually, they are pulled down into the thickest part of Earth's atmosphere. The pieces of space debris heat up and disintegrate as they travel at high speed through the atmosphere. Very occasionally, however, pieces of debris survive re-entry and land on Earth!

SPACE OBJECTS FACT FILE

Space debris that's orbiting at around 500 miles (800 km) will suffer orbital decay within decades. Objects orbiting above this height may remain in space for 100 years or more.

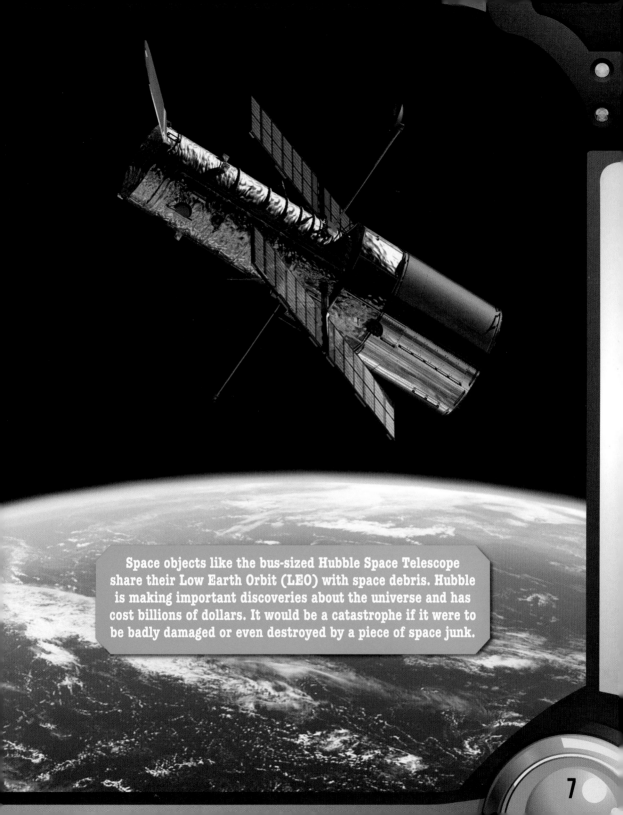

Space objects like the bus-sized Hubble Space Telescope share their Low Earth Orbit (LEO) with space debris. Hubble is making important discoveries about the universe and has cost billions of dollars. It would be a catastrophe if it were to be badly damaged or even destroyed by a piece of space junk.

WHAT'S UP THERE?

There are many different types of space debris orbiting Earth.

When spacecraft are launched, they must be blasted into orbit around Earth. Some sections of the rocket fall back to Earth soon after launch. Others remain attached to the spacecraft and only separate once the spacecraft is beyond Earth's atmosphere. Then, with their mission complete, the rocket sections go into orbit around Earth as space debris.

Tool bag

This photo shows astronaut Heidemarie Stefanyshyn-Piper's tool bag floating away from the International Space Station (ISS). The astronaut dropped the bag as she carried out repairs to the ISS.

Some of the largest objects classified as space debris are satellites that are no longer in operation. These objects, which can be the size of cars, may have malfunctioned or been shut down once their work was done. A damaged or retired satellite is no longer useful, but it can remain in orbit for many decades.

In the 1980s and 1990s, **cosmonauts** living aboard the Mir space station released bags of their garbage into space. There have even been cases of astronauts losing objects while carrying out spacewalks. This "lost-and-found" of outer space includes cameras, a pair of pliers, a tool bag, and even a glove.

SPACE OBJECTS FACT FILE

NASA's *Vanguard 1* satellite was launched in 1958 and stopped operating in the 1960s. It's been estimated, however, that the defunct satellite may continue to orbit Earth for another 200 years or more!

HOW BIG IS SPACE DEBRIS?

NASA's figure of an estimated 500,000 pieces of space debris includes only pieces of junk that are larger than a marble.

Included in the 500,000 pieces are around 20,000 that are bigger than a softball. These pieces of space debris are large enough to track and monitor. They may include old satellites or large fragments of shattered rockets.

In addition to the 500,000 pieces of debris that are marble-sized or larger, there are many millions of much smaller fragments of junk. As pieces of space debris break apart over time or even collide with each other, far more tiny fragments are made than bigger pieces. It's just the same as when you break a drinking glass. You might end up with four or five large shards of glass, but hundreds of dust-sized pieces.

Just because a piece of debris is tiny, however, doesn't mean it's not dangerous. When it's traveling at 17,500 miles per hour (28,000 km/h), even a fleck of paint can damage a spacecraft!

SPACE OBJECTS FACT FILE

Satellites launched by the **Soviet Union** in the 1970s and 1980s contain a coolant liquid. This liquid can escape from a defunct satellite and form droplets in space. Even this liquid debris can cause damage if it impacts with another space object.

In space, something as small as this bolt could cause damage to a spacecraft, such as the *Soyuz* that carries astronauts to the International Space Station (ISS).

Soyuz spacecraft

TRACKING SPACE DEBRIS

In the United States, NASA, the Department of Defense, and the United States Space Surveillance Network all carry out work to catalog and track objects that are orbiting Earth and are larger than a softball.

Some of these objects are active satellites or space telescopes. Most are pieces of space debris. It's also possible to track smaller pieces, some of them just the size of a Ping-Pong ball, but not all of these can be watched. In order to figure out the number of small pieces of space debris orbiting Earth, NASA gathers as much data as possible and then estimates a total number.

Tracking space debris allows scientists to know the position of all large pieces of space junk and their future orbital paths. This helps scientists predict whether an object will collide with a spacecraft or the ISS. They can also predict where and when an object might decay and re-enter Earth's atmosphere. If this happens, a warning can be sent to the military of countries worldwide so that no nation mistakes the debris for a missile attack by another country.

SPACE OBJECTS FACT FILE

Not all objects that orbit Earth are made by humans. Some small natural space objects, such as rocky **meteoroids**, are also in orbit. Meteoroids are small pieces of rock that have broken away from much bigger **asteroids**.

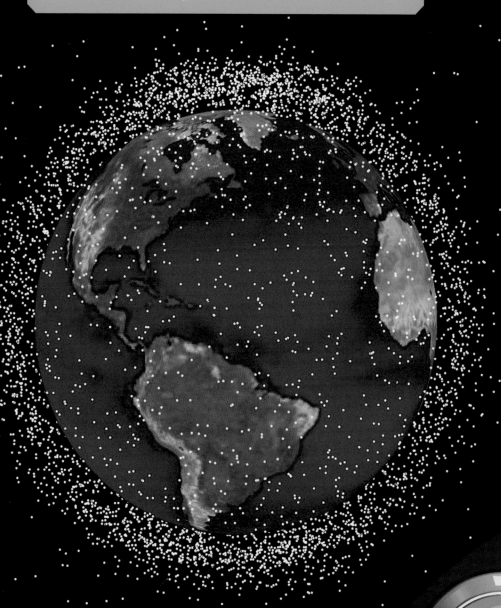

This image was created by NASA to show the objects in Low Earth Orbit that are being tracked. About 95 percent of them are space debris. The positions of the objects are true to life, but the size of the objects is not to scale because they have been enlarged to make them visible.

ANTI-SATELLITE WEAPONS

Large quantities of space debris have been created by the deliberate destruction of satellites during tests of anti-satellite weapons (ASATs).

Nations develop ASATs in order to destroy their enemies' satellites. For example, a satellite might be targeted because it's being used to spy on another nation. Today, most nations do not carry out ASAT testing because it creates space debris. For many years, however, some nations, including the United States and the Soviet Union, tested ASATs by blowing up their own defunct satellites.

In 2007, China carried out an anti-satellite weapons test by blowing up an old Chinese weather satellite. Within hours, a cloud of debris from the explosion spread out in orbit around Earth. The destruction of the satellite created more than 3,000 pieces of debris that are large enough to track. Scientists estimate that it also created more than 150,000 pieces of debris that are larger than marbles.

SPACE OBJECTS FACT FILE

China's deliberate destruction of its weather satellite in 2007 created more space debris than any single earlier event. Scientists have calculated that most of the debris will be orbiting Earth for more than 100 years.

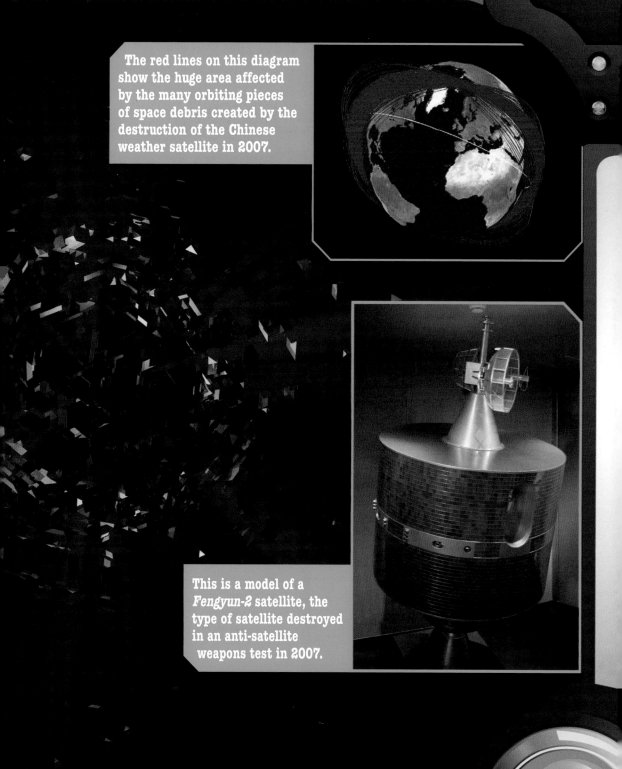

The red lines on this diagram show the huge area affected by the many orbiting pieces of space debris created by the destruction of the Chinese weather satellite in 2007.

This is a model of a *Fengyun-2* satellite, the type of satellite destroyed in an anti-satellite weapons test in 2007.

GARBAGE COLLISIONS

As the many thousands of pieces of space debris orbit Earth, they often collide with each other. In 2009, a collision between an active U.S. satellite and a large piece of space junk took place in Low Earth Orbit (LEO).

On February 10, 2009, the U.S. *Iridium 33* satellite was orbiting Earth and transmitting telephone signals. Suddenly, it collided with a defunct Russian military satellite, *Kosmos-2251*. The collision took place 490 miles (789 km) above the remote Taymyr Peninsula in Siberia. The two objects were traveling at high speed, and the impact happened at a combined speed of 26,000 miles per hour (42,000 km/h). Both satellites were instantly destroyed and quickly became a cloud of orbiting debris.

By 2012, NASA reported that more than 2,000 large pieces of debris from the incident were being tracked. The smaller fragments were too tiny and too many to track or calculate!

SPACE OBJECTS FACT FILE

The region of space where the 2009 collision took place is one of the most crowded. There is more space debris orbiting at around 500 miles (800 km) above Earth's surface than at any other height.

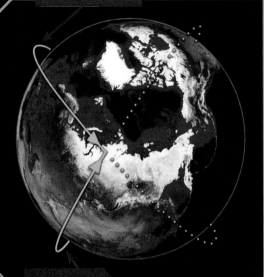

Kosmos-2251

Iridium 33

This illustration shows the position of the collision between *Iridium 33* and *Kosmos-2251*.

This illustration shows the debris clouds 20 minutes after the collision.

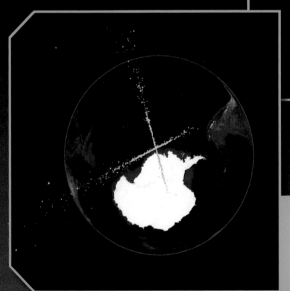

This illustration shows debris in orbit 50 minutes after the collision.

DAMAGE TO SPACECRAFT

If data shows that a collision is likely between a large piece of space debris and a manned spacecraft, telescope, or active satellite, an avoidance maneuver is carried out.

A small change is made to the orbital pathway of the spacecraft or object that's in danger. The avoidance maneuver usually takes place several hours before the expected collision. It's not possible, however, for spacecraft to avoid collisions with tiny, non-trackable pieces of space garbage or small natural objects such as meteoroids.

During their missions, NASA's space shuttles suffered many small impacts from pieces of space debris. A number of space shuttle windows had to be replaced after missions because they were damaged. When the windows were analyzed, scientists discovered that some of the damage was caused by flecks of paint!

The Long Duration Exposure Facility (LDEF) was a bus-sized satellite that spent nearly six years in Low Earth Orbit (LEO) studying space. When it returned to Earth at the end of its mission, scientists found more than 20,000 small debris impacts on the satellite.

SPACE OBJECTS FACT FILE

Studying the size and number of impacts from space debris on spacecraft that return to Earth allows scientists to estimate how much debris is out there.

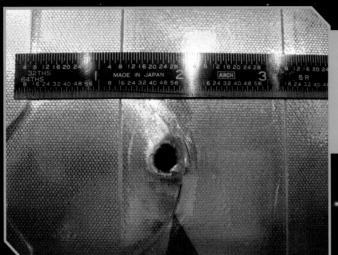

This small impact hole on the space shuttle *Endeavour*'s radiator panel was caused by a piece of space debris.

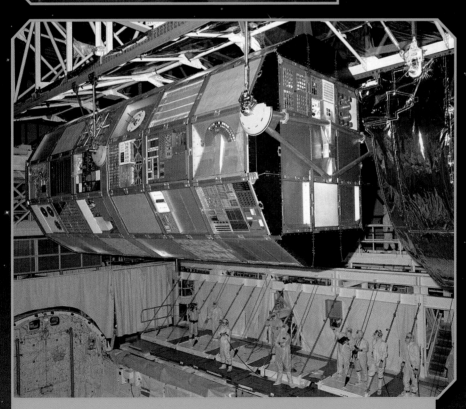

NASA scientists watch as the Long Duration Exposure Facility (LDEF) is lifted from the space shuttle *Columbia* on the satellite's return to Earth.

SAFE INSIDE THE PIZZA BOX

The International Space Station (ISS) is the size of a football field. As it moves around Earth in a Low Earth Orbit (LEO), it presents a very large target for space debris.

With as many as seven astronauts aboard at any one time, a collision with space garbage could be catastrophic!

NASA creates an imaginary box, or exclusion zone, around the ISS. The imaginary box is about one mile (1.6 km) deep, 30 miles (48 km) long, and 30 miles (48 km) wide. The flat, square shape of this "safe area" has earned it the nickname of the "pizza box." If a tracked piece of space debris may be on course to enter the box, safety precautions are taken.

If there is enough advance warning, the orbit of the ISS can be adjusted. In some cases, the ISS remains in position but the crew takes refuge in the Soyuz spacecraft that is permanently docked with the space station. Then, if a collision were to seriously damage the ISS, the crew can immediately take off and return to Earth.

SPACE OBJECTS FACT FILE

On March 24, 2012, a piece of the *Kosmos-2251* satellite (destroyed in a collision in 2009) came close to the International Space Station (ISS). As the debris passed, the six-member crew waited in two *Soyuz* spacecraft in case an evacuation was needed.

The International Space Station (ISS) is a huge structure, as shown in this illustration.

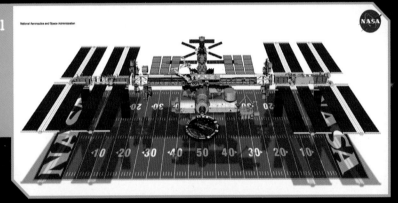

A *Soyuz* spacecraft docked with the International Space Station (ISS).

SHIELDS FOR SPACECRAFT

Tracking space debris and issuing warnings of potential collisions is one way to keep spacecraft safe. Another way to protect spacecraft is to use shielding.

When a marble-size piece of debris collides with a spacecraft, it's like a hand grenade hitting the spacecraft's exterior. Normally, protecting against this type of force would require the panels of a spacecraft to be built from very thick metal. In order to launch a spacecraft, however, it must be as light as possible.

One way to achieve strong but lightweight shielding was invented by American scientist Fred Whipple in the 1940s. A section of Whipple shielding can be made from two thin layers of metal instead of one thick layer. A projectile such as a piece of space debris hits the shield. It pierces the thin outer layer of metal, but the impact slows the projectile and breaks it into smaller fragments. The small fragments then hit the thicker, inner layer of metal, but only have the speed and power to do limited damage.

SPACE OBJECTS FACT FILE

As space technology has advanced, Whipple shields have developed, too. Today's shields have additional layers of high-strength, lightweight materials such as Kevlar. These fabric layers help reduce the impact when a projectile hits the multilayered shield.

In a laboratory test, a pea-sized bullet was shot at a section of Whipple shielding at a speed of 4 miles (7 km) per second.

Bullet hole in aluminum

The bullet tore through the shield's outer padded fabric layer and through the thin outer layer of aluminum.

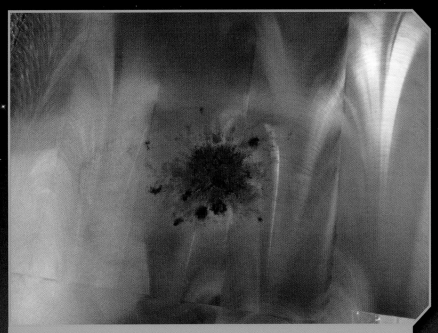

The thick inner layer of aluminum shows scorch marks from the shattered bullet, but it is not damaged.

DOWN TO EARTH

Even though there is an enormous amount of debris in space, it rarely falls to Earth, and there are no records of a person being hit or killed by falling space garbage.

When pieces of space debris do fall back to Earth, they usually burn up in the atmosphere. If a piece of space junk survives re-entry, however, the chances are it will land in an ocean or lake. That's because about 70 percent of Earth is covered with water. It might also come down in one of Earth's vast wildernesses, such as the Canadian tundra or Australian outback.

NASA estimates that on average one large piece of space debris has landed back on Earth each year for the past 50 years. In January 2001, this happened in Saudi Arabia. A section of a rocket used to launch a U.S. satellite in 1993 came crashing back to Earth. Thankfully, it landed in a desert where there were no people or buildings to harm.

SPACE OBJECTS FACT FILE

In 1979, NASA's defunct Skylab space station re-entered Earth's atmosphere. The space station disintegrated, and only small pieces of debris came down over the Indian Ocean and remote areas of western Australia.

This photo shows the rocket section that landed in a Saudi Arabian desert in 2001.

This large piece of space garbage is a propellant tank from a Delta 2 rocket. It landed near Georgetown, Texas, in January 1997.

A RUNAWAY PROBLEM?

Even if no more completely new pieces of debris were to go into space, the total number of pieces would still continue to grow. That's because existing pieces of space garbage orbiting Earth collide with each other.

If one piece of football-sized debris hits a defunct satellite, the satellite can be smashed into thousands of pieces. Those pieces then go on to collide with others. Like a chain reaction, the amount of debris grows.

The more garbage there is in orbit around Earth, the harder it becomes to protect satellites, telescopes, and the International Space Station (ISS). It also becomes much harder to find safe pathways for spacecraft, such as *Soyuz*, to use when in flight.

Today, space organizations around the world are committed to protecting the space environment and reducing the amount of space debris they produce. From rockets that do not leave unwanted sections in orbit to actually removing large pieces of garbage from space, there is a real drive to keep space safe for future generations to explore.

SPACE OBJECTS FACT FILE

In 1978, NASA scientist Donald J. Kessler put forward a shocking theory about the future. Known as Kessler Syndrome, the theory says that one day the amount of space debris around our planet could cascade out of control, making space travel too dangerous for centuries.

This illustration shows a collision between space debris and a satellite.

THE BIG SPACE CLEANUP

It's going to take more than a vacuum cleaner, but scientists and engineers worldwide are looking for ways to clean up space.

One idea is to capture large pieces of debris with a type of harpoon. This ancient hunting weapon has been used for thousands of years to catch animals such as fish and whales.

In space, a spacecraft would approach a defunct satellite or some other large piece of debris. Then, a large, powerful, spear-like harpoon would be released from the spacecraft to penetrate the satellite. Just like a hunting harpoon, the spear would be attached to a tether connected to the spacecraft. Once the satellite was captured, it could be reeled in and then carried back to Earth in the spacecraft for safe disposal or even recycling.

When we look up into space at night, we can't see our space junkyard, but it's there. Fixing the problem will need innovative ideas and exciting new technology. Tomorrow's space scientists, engineers, and astronauts will be kept very busy tackling the big space cleanup.

SPACE OBJECTS FACT FILE

Satellites could be fitted with a large, thin, parachute-like sail. Once a satellite was no longer in use, its sail would be deployed. The open sail would cause drag through the atmosphere. This would slow the satellite, causing it to drop toward Earth and burn up in the atmosphere.

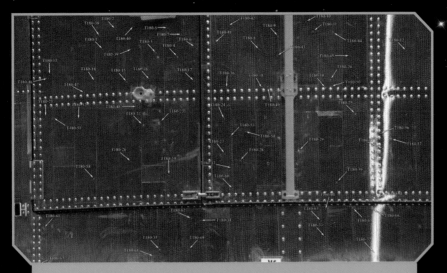

The yellow arrows on these panels from the Hubble Space Telescope show multiple impacts from small pieces of space debris. What ideas can be developed for capturing tiny pieces of space garbage?

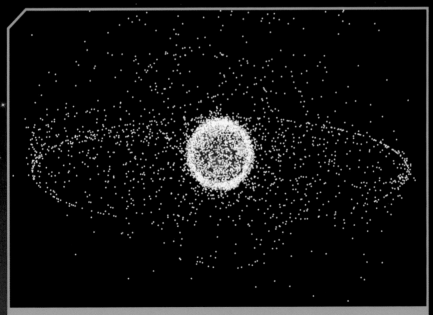

This NASA illustration shows the space debris problem beyond Low Earth Orbit (LEO).

GLOSSARY

asteroids
(AS-tuh-roydz) Rocky objects orbiting the Sun and ranging in size from a few feet (m) to hundreds of miles (km) in diameter.

atmosphere
(AT-muh-sfeer) The layer of gases surrounding a planet, moon, or star.

cosmonauts
(KAHZ-muh-nawtz) Astronauts from Russia, and before 1991, from the Soviet Union.

Kevlar
(KEV-lar) A high strength, artificial fiber used in the construction of planes, racing cars, helmets, and fireproof protective clothing.

meteoroids
(MEE-tee-uh-roydz) Small particles or fragments that have broken free from an asteroid.

NASA
(NAS-ah) The National Aeronautics and Space Administration, an agency in the United States that studies space and builds spacecraft.

orbiting
(OR-bih-ting) Moving, or traveling, around another object in a curved path.

satellites
(SA-tih-lytz) Objects that orbit another object in space, such as a planet. A satellite may be naturally occurring, such as a moon, or an artificial satellite used for transmitting television or cell phone signals.

Soviet Union
(SOH-vee-et YOON-yun)
A former nation made up of a group of republics in parts of Europe and Asia. The Soviet Union broke up in 1991, creating a group of independent nations, including Russia, Ukraine, Kazakhstan, and Georgia.

space telescopes
(SPAYSS TEL-uh-scopes)
Telescopes that are launched into space and orbit Earth. Space telescopes fly above Earth's atmosphere, which allows them to see distant objects in space more clearly because their view is not obscured by gases and dust in Earth's atmosphere.

WEBSITES

Due to the changing nature of Internet links, PowerKids Press has developed an online list of websites related to the subject of this book. This site is updated regularly. Please use this link to access the list: www.powerkidslinks.com/ois/garbage

READ MORE

Poolos, Christine. *What Is an Object in the Sky?*
New York: Rosen Publishing Group, 2015.

Silverman, Buffy. *Exploring Dangers in Space: Asteroids,
Space Junk, and More.* Minneapolis, MN: Lerner
Publishing Group, 2011.

Weil, Ann. *Space Disasters.* Costa Mesa, CA:
Saddleback Educational Publishing, 2013.